HRH THE PRINCE OF WALES WATERCOLOURS

C/91

HRH THE PRINCE OF WALES WATERCOLOURS

A Bulfinch Press Book

LITTLE, BROWN AND COMPANY

Boston   Toronto   London

CONTENTS

THE WATERCOLOURS

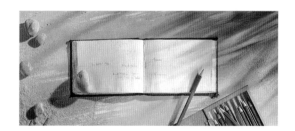

FOREWORD BY HER MAJESTY

Queen Elizabeth The Queen Mother

One of the most difficult things in the world must surely be to write dispassionately about a member of one's own family. This difficulty is compounded by the fact that I find myself writing about my grandson's painting abilities so must avoid any undue bias.

That said, I am delighted that this book is being published, and it is nice to think that a wider audience will now have a chance to see some of the watercolours painted by my grandson in many different parts of the world.

Ever since he was a small boy Prince Charles has taken an interest in his surroundings, and has developed his powers of observation to the point where painting became a necessary and vital expression of that interest. Perhaps he has been fortunate that from an early age he was able to roam the beautiful hills in Scotland and watch the changing colours as the clouds rolled by; to enjoy the quality of light on the great marshes of Norfolk, and, later on, bask in the beauties of Tuscany.

After advice from teachers and friends, it is interesting to see how my grandson's technique and ability have gradually changed and improved through the years, so that now he has developed a definite style of his own. Some of the paintings are delightfully evocative, especially of those scenes I know so well, and I think that it is apparent just how much his heart and soul has gone into their production.

I hope from my heart that this book will give as much pleasure to those who cast their eyes on it as my beloved grandson's enthusiastic painting activities have given to his affectionate grandmother.

Elizabeth R

These are the paintings of a traveller with time ever at his elbow, but then nearly all painting is fraught with urgency, with the balancing of opportunity, energy and talent against the constant movement of the elements. A grasp of the economics of painting is essential and clearly the Prince is a realist.

First the size of the paintings; they appear small, almost very small when one thinks of the usual watercolour, but even great painters like Turner, Constable and Delacroix produced many works on this scale. Indeed looking at these pictures, I am reminded of the watercolours Delacroix made on his Moroccan trip (for me one of the greatest series of watercolours). Working on this scale makes for an immediacy which becomes more difficult on a larger one where wash is laid upon wash to achieve strength, thus rendering less spontaneous the brilliant delicacy of watercolour which is its chief virtue.

Then the balance of drawing to painting; how much of the bones of landscape and form of the architecture need to be defined before the plunge into colour? The eye is steadied by preliminary drawing, but it might also be said that some of the initial head of steam is lost. Against this must be set the painter's constant desire to train himself for the long haul, the finished masterpiece where trial and error will not blunt the impetus, but deepen and enrich it. To 'fill in' a pencil drawing is often to extract the fizz, the first inspiration, and one can end up with neither a decent drawing nor much of the racy quality which is watercolour.

In painting number 17 of Balmoral the balance of preliminary drawing and painting is well managed. There is caution too, a caution which comes not from timidity but from respect and humility before landscape of such grandeur as well as his knowledge and love of painting. This is a landscape the Prince knows and must have observed at every season and at most times of the day since his many outdoor pursuits demand periods of stillness and the facing of inclement weather rather than 'it's a nice afternoon, let's go out and do some sketching'. In these works we see how sensitive he is to the siting of buildings in a landscape. In painting number 18 of Balmoral, the hills tower above the castle, rendering it small and puny, yet the rich complexity of its architecture is not lost. Its decorative fragility is nicely, skilfully, set against the warm colour of the near trees and the cool green of the distant ones.

Cool and warm colours; the sorting out of this problem is central to good colour if painting is to be more than the transposition of colour from paintbox to paper. Too often painters are urged, commended, to use colour 'adventurously' and this usually means that the picture will be painted without much reference to the subject before the painter's eye. I believe that a sense of colour can only develop by humble observation; variety and richness of colour have to be fought for.

In the Prince's Brig O'Dee, painting number 41, the use of warm and cool colours is skilful. The mass of mountain is drawn in a warm grey and modelled with a warmer colour which marries

Brig O'Dee, Dee Valley

excellently with the pinkish brown underlying the trees, giving a vibrance when the cool green tree shapes are washed over.

The view from Seguret towards Avignon, painting number 52, achieves space with almost an Edward Lear touch – the cyprus trees leading the eye easily into the distance. The Prince has a nice instinct for knowing when patience is required and dash has to be tempered with labour as in the line of fencing in painting number 28. In painting number 69 the pause between the summary washes which catch the feel of building, desert and sky, while apertures and battlements are carefully picked out, gives delicacy and grandeur to the whole.

Clearly the relationship between architecture and landscape has long been in the Prince's mind. In my own case, when confronted by the complexity of landscape I pounce upon any man-made shape with relief, for there is something understandable and, perhaps, working out from building to domesticized shapes found in garden, orchard or field, a way might be found to understand the chaos of the rest of the landscape. Architecture set in landscape forces one to consider more acutely the balance of roof to roof, the height related to length, the punctuation of chimney, window and door-way and how comfortably the building sits on hillside or plain. The drift of buildings in the Prince's Norfolk painting number 7 are seen with an architectural eye, as also is the view of Prince Albert's Kitchen Garden Buildings, Windsor. Here it

Looking towards Mar Lodge, Dee Valley

is interesting to reflect upon the great variety of styles and scales of building which have formed the background of the Prince's life; cottage, stable, dairy, garden building as well as the palatial splendour of monarchical life. How well is the character of Allt-na-Giubsaich Lodge at Balmoral grasped despite wobbly perspective.

Here and there in the pictures can be seen the signs of rain, physical signs, the speckled blotch and perhaps the bonus of good luck when, for a reason beyond the painter's control, colours mingle magically for a moment and the decision must be made to preserve this effect or plod on. In the Dee Valley painting, number 37, a sensitive eye has said 'enough', I must keep this 'lovely mess'.

The jump from Scotland to Tuscany produces interesting results. Brilliant light does not necessarily increase colour, often it drains it away, olive trees are a muted green compared to the rich foliage which covers the hills of Balmoral, but the grandeur of scale is comparable. In the view of Cacchiano from Brolio, painting number 46, is felt the excitement of a new subject. Here the little groups of buildings are fallen upon, nailed down with pen and ink but sensibly some-what unnailed when the colour unifies the components of the view.

In the Port Suez picture, number 68, tone is sensitively felt, the white superstructure of the ship carefully retained as untouched paper and the accurate drawing of the vessel giving weight and conviction. A real sense of heat is achieved.

Does one see a preference for hill, mountain and rugged landscape in this collection? Perhaps this appreciation of high space comes from the valued moments of release from the prison of office, a blessed breathing space when contemplation and action may go hand in hand. Certainly there is nothing forced about the Prince's pictures. There are no pretensions. Much applause could have been won by what is termed a more 'adventurous' approach, a tearing up of that particular pea patch sorely in need of rest, care and cultivation. In the tiny work, number 7, 'Farm

Farm buildings, Norfolk

buildings, Norfolk', the Prince nails down all the requirements of a picture; relationships, space, colour and atmosphere are set down without hesitation.

The Prince is an amateur in the best sense of the word – as were many of our best architects and painters. He works for the love of it; seriously, modestly, with much thought as well as appetite. The Prince has edge, his remarks on the most important of the visual arts, architecture, have left an indelible mark, breathing life into a discussion which seemed to have given up the ghost in the face of seemingly unstoppable horror.

Throughout the pictures there is a sense of urgency combined with a determination to stop and look, that amounts to a *necessity* to paint. For it is not just a matter of recording (after all, where the Prince is, cameras are never far away), but of examining, taking in and considering the visual world – and then responding in the medium of watercolour. With affairs of state blowing him hither and thither across the globe and these matters making him privy to much which controls our landscape, seascape and townscape, I rejoice greatly, as a professional painter, in the fact that the finger which the Prince puts into so many pies is that of a dedicated painter.

INTRODUCTION BY HIS ROYAL HIGHNESS

The Prince of Wales

I must confess that no-one could have been more surprised than me to discover that a courageous (or, perhaps, foolhardy!) publisher wished to compile a book of my watercolour sketches. When I first started dabbling in watercolours, over twenty years ago, any thought of such an eventuality would have seemed utterly ludicrous.

I took up painting entirely because I found photography less than satisfying. Quite simply, I experienced an overwhelming urge to express what I saw through the medium of watercolour and to convey that almost 'inner' sense of texture which is impossible to achieve via photography. I very quickly discovered how incredibly difficult it is to paint well in such a spontaneous medium, and the feeling of frustration at not being able to achieve on paper the image that your eye has presented you with is intense!

Looking back now at those first sketches I did, I am appalled by how bad they are. But, nevertheless, the great thing about painting is that you are making your own individual interpretation of whatever view you have chosen. Because it obliges you to sit down and make a careful observation of the selected subject, you discover so much more about it than by just pointing a camera and arriving at a result which is probably almost identical to somebody else's photograph. As a result, you become increasingly aware of things that may have escaped your attention previously - things like the quality of light and shade, of tone and texture and of the shape of buildings in relation to the landscape. It all requires the most intense concentration and, consequently, is one of the most relaxing and therapeutic exercises I know. In fact, in my case, I find it transports me into another dimension which, quite literally, refreshes parts of the soul which other activities can't reach....

After twenty years of practising quietly and of pressing dreadfully bad sketches upon unfortunate relations or friends, I was somewhat taken aback to receive an invitation in 1988 to exhibit some of my watercolour sketches, following a visit to Raphael's house in the Italian town of Urbino, in that same house. My initial reaction was one of amused astonishment and I decided to decline the invitation. However, I thought a bit more about the idea, talked to a few professional artists whom I know and admire and, finally, came to the conclusion that it was worth the risk. The risk, of course, was of ridicule from the professional art critics. I am, after all, under no illusion that my sketches represent great art or a burgeoning talent! They represent, more than anything else, my particular form of 'photograph album' and, as such, mean a great deal to me. The risk was worthwhile, it seemed to me, because I felt that such an exhibition could perhaps be a small contribution towards the further development of an ever-warmer relationship between Great Britain and Italy. I must explain here that I have a passion for Italy, her people and her countryside. The way in which art quite naturally seems to invade every aspect of life produces, for me, an atmosphere that is totally irresistible and utterly unique. It was because of this passion that I finally overcame my extreme reluctance to send anything to an exhibition. I am sure others who paint will understand how hard it is to part with something into which, when suitably inspired, you have poured your heart and soul, but in this case I felt that to exhibit would also be a token of my warmest gratitude to the Government and people of Italy for

the hospitality and friendship they have always shown to me.

One very encouraging result of this exhibition was that a substantial sum was made available to the British Institute of Florence, of which I am Patron, and which is dedicated to strengthening the cultural ties between Italy and Great Britain.

Following the exhibition at Urbino in May 1990, it was suggested to me in my capacity as President of the Salisbury Cathedral Spire Appeal that one way of raising money for the restoration of this great medieval monument was to hold a similar exhibition in Salisbury. This duly took place in September 1990 and I was thrilled to have been able to make this personal contribution to the Cathedral appeal.

And now, to my continuing surprise, there are plans being formulated for further exhibitions to be held in various parts of the world. For me, one of the most important objectives of these exhibitions, and of this publication, (apart from, I hope, giving some pleasure to those who see them or read the book) is that all the proceeds will be donated to The Prince of Wales's Charities Trust. This will enable me to help support many of the projects and worthwhile causes which so badly need funding.

I have already tried to describe how I came to take up painting and what it means to me, but my publisher insists that I should say something about the tuition, if any, that I received, and about the methods and equipment I use!

Years ago, when I first experienced this unaccountable urge to paint, I remember asking a famous Norfolk artist, Ted Seago, whom I had known since I was a child, if he would give me some lessons. His response was that he didn't really know how to teach, but that if I watched him paint in his studio he would describe what he was doing as he did it. I stood behind him, lost in wonder, as a stunning watercolour emerged as if by magic – and entirely from his memory. I learnt absolutely nothing, except that to paint well in watercolour is far more difficult than it looks, requires the acquisition of technical skills born of endless trial and error and is much assisted by a liberal helping of innate talent!

I have been lucky enough to obtain wonderfully useful hints from such accomplished artists as Sir Hugh Casson who, on his own admission, sketches with pen and watercolour in the same way that other people hum tunes! His critical and constructive encouragement has been enormously important to me. John Ward is another of the major influences in my sketching life. I have long admired his consummate style and dexterity and so, when he kindly agreed to accompany us on a tour of Italy in 1985 in order to record some of the places and events, I availed myself of the opportunity to paint with him and to learn from the experience. He introduced me to the delights of using tinted paper and white chalk, but looking back on my efforts then makes me deeply depressed!

One of the things I feel strongly about is the need to keep the Royal Collection alive through the commissioning of works of art by artists and craftsmen. One way to achieve this is by taking an artist on official tours abroad so that a worthwhile record is available for posterity. In the very odd moments that are available to me during these rather hectic tours I am sometimes able to extract some useful tuition from the accompanying artist. Amongst this number are included such painters as Martin Yeoman, Peter Kuhfeld and Derek Hill. I owe a lot, too, to Bryan Organ who tried hard to give me a few hints on painting still life. I seem to recall a memorable mackerel which caused me immense difficulty!

As far as the equipment I use is concerned, I tend to employ the barest minimum. This is chiefly because I prefer to paint in the open air and this usually involves carrying a paint bag on long walks. As a result this bag is invariably in a dreadful mess! Whether I am painting outside, in the summer, or inside, in January, I always use one of the small Winsor and Newton paintboxes and a selection of Roberson paint brushes. A pencil, an indispensable eraser, a pencil-sharpener and several Kleenex tissues complete the picture. As I said, the majority of my sketches have been made outside, in all weathers (hence some of them have been affected by rain!) and, as a result, I find it easier and simpler to paint on fairly small pieces of paper. Some of the sketches are, I fear, rather unfinished — usually because I have run out of time or because, in places like Italy or the Middle East, I have become embarrassed at keeping the police waiting for too long! My sketches are, by necessity and probably intention, immediate and very amateur. I find that if I am able to paint at least once every day for, say, five days consecutively, then I become considerably better. It is so much a question of practice, and that is something of which I am rather short! It is, perhaps, worth emphasizing that my life being what it is, I tend to have long gaps between being able to paint. Invariably these gaps amount to three months at a time which means that I am always having to get back into practice and to re-learn hard-won techniques. The reason for so many sketches being of the landscape around Balmoral or Sandringham is purely because the best chance for painting is in April, August and September, and then again in January. The ones of Italy have to be squeezed into my short, annual cultural visits to that country in May when I am also trying to visit interesting sites, towns and houses. Any others derive from even hastier and un-practised sketches grabbed in the margins of official tours.

I have tried in these pages to convey something of the part that painting plays in my life. In many ways it helps to keep me reasonably sane, and if it doesn't appeal to the critics, then it's just too bad! I only hope that those who are rash enough to thumb through this book may be helped to discover what infinite beauty and delight there is in the details of God's creation, and how vitally important it is — if we are to preserve the essential elements of this beauty and delight — that man-made structures and landscaping features are fitted into the overall picture with sensitivity and vision. It seems to me that we can't go far wrong if we try to aspire to the principle that whatever development takes place should owe something to the well-trained artist's eye.

ENGLISH SCENES

1

WINDSOR CASTLE

Berkshire 1990

Whenever I am tempted to do a sketch at Windsor I am reminded of generations of great artists who have painted the castle and its surroundings over the past nine hundred years, and I hardly dare pick up my brush.... Just looking at what Turner and Sandby made of the castle practically forces me to give up the unequal struggle, But not *quite*...!

In April last year I sat down to draw this aspect of the castle. No sooner had I got half way than an immense black cloud stole on to the scene and the heavens opened. Sheltering pathetically under a leafless tree, I waited for the huge shower to pass. As it drifted away to the east, the sun, by now declining in the west, suddenly emerged from behind the angry, black cloud and turned it into a dramatic dark purple backdrop to the illuminated towers of the castle. It was a passing instant that I printed on my mind so that I could return to the sketch once I had gone indoors.

Although this is a very inadequate representation of the castle, it reminds me of a dramatic moment in time when Sir Geoffrey Wyattville's towers and turrets were shown to their best advantage. It also reminds me of those childhood days when my sister and I used to explore the castle and find all sorts of fascinating places on which to exercise our imagination.

2

PRINCE ALBERT'S KITCHEN GARDEN BUILDINGS

Windsor, Berkshire 1989

My great-great-great grandfather, Prince Albert, was clearly a man of remarkable energy, ability and vision. It is extraordinary to think that he died at the age of forty two – the same age as I am now – having accomplished as much as he did. Windsor, Balmoral and Osborne House, on the Isle of Wight, are a testament to his energy and his attention to detail. At both Windsor and Balmoral he built what can only be described as model farms for their period. He and Queen Victoria built many cottages of considerable character on both estates, and while being a man of cultivated tastes he was also a remarkable innovator. As a result, he seems to have been almost universally misunderstood by most people in this country during his lifetime!

The buildings in this sketch were a part of the new kitchen garden he laid out at Windsor. I painted this from within the garden at Frogmore in the Home Park during an Easter weekend. I particularly liked the horizontal bands of colour made up of the sky, the distant trees, the cherry trees coming into bud and the hedge in the foreground. I cannot pretend it is anything but amateur, but it was an extremely good exercise in observation of detail and kept me out of mischief!

3

LOOKING TOWARDS NORTH CREAKE

Holkham, Norfolk 1990

This is a lovely, rolling piece of Norfolk just outside the great Capability Brown park at Holkham. Without a doubt that park is one of the most spectacular feats of landscape design in this country. Its sheer scale is so impressive, and the planting is second to none. When you think that Mr Brown would never have seen the results of his labours, it is remarkable what he achieved. For me, one of the greatest features of the park is the clumps of ilex trees which, so the story goes, grew from the seeds that were collected from the packing cases in which Roman sculpture, protected by ilex branches, had been transported to Holkham in the eighteenth century. One day I hope to paint in the park at Holkham, but meanwhile I have been content with this view towards North Creake!

C'90

SANDRINGHAM HOUSE

Norfolk 1991

Until I tried to paint Sandringham I thought Balmoral was difficult enough.... But Sandringham is in a league of its own, as I discovered the moment I started to draw the house. It is a veritable minefield of gables, bow windows, parapets, balustrades, towers, cupolas and gigantic chimneys. Trying to get the perspective right was an intriguing challenge in itself, and I'm afraid I haven't succeeded. I made life more difficult for myself by selecting a pretty impossible angle from which to do the painting, but I thought it would be more interesting than most others.

This painting took me days to complete. I kept returning to a spot beside the lake, much to the astonishment of the patrolling policemen, and added parts of the building piece by piece. There was only one fine day during the time I was doing this, so I had to remember where all the shadows were and put them in when I got back to the house. Painting in all the details gave me spots in front of the eyes and architectural hallucinations, but many would probably say I have had those for some time....

Looking at Sandringham makes me wonder at what my forbears as Prince of Wales were able to achieve in days gone by. How things have changed!

C '91

5 & 6

VIEWS OVER HILLINGTON ON A JANUARY AFTERNOON

Norfolk 1990

Both these sketches were the result of going for a walk on a January afternoon at Sandringham and stopping to admire a favourite view from one of the only pieces of rising ground in that part of Norfolk. This favourite view is always full of surprises and on this occasion the setting winter sun created the sort of dramatic display which had me fumbling desperately for my paint box before it all vanished in a trice.

I sat with my back against an oak tree, my fingers becoming ever more numb from the cold, but consumed by a sense of impassioned and happy urgency to record the almost ethereal demonstration that was taking place in front of me. This was one of those special occasions when I could actually feel the inner appreciation of the beauty of the moment passing like an electric current through the brush in my hand. I was totally absorbed. I was in another world, or another dimension; all sense of time evaporated.

The second sketch was completed virtually in the dark and from memory. I had to work so fast that it was almost impossible for the paint to dry in those cold conditions, and so it has run here and there in various directions! The foreground in fact consists of a stubble field which, amazingly, glowed orange and copper in the embers of that dying January sun.

FARM BUILDINGS

Norfolk 1987

Believe it or not, this is the tiny sketch which I sent in, under an assumed name and with somebody else's address, to the Royal Academy of Art's Summer Exhibition in 1988. To my absolute amazement it was accepted. In fact I suspect it was put to one side because the judges were undecided as to whether to reject it or not and it was finally hung because it was so small it was quite easy to find a piece of wall to put it on! It had been cut down drastically from a bigger sketch and I was completely overwhelmed that it had actually ended up on the wall of that august artistic institution. If anyone thinks it might have gone to my head they are wrong because I had three paintings rejected by the judges for the 1990 Summer Exhibition!

I always felt that I had made a bit of a mess of this sketch. The paint had run all over the place in a thoroughly uncontrolled fashion and the buildings hadn't been drawn very well, but there is nevertheless something quite pleasing, perhaps, in those pale, rather translucent colours which you do find in Norfolk on certain occasions.

This may easily become the first and only painting I ever have in the Royal Academy Summer Exhibition!

-0

8

COTTAGES IN THE SNOW

Sandringham, Norfolk 1987

I decided to be more daring with this sketch and to do it without any preliminary drawing, merely attacking the paper directly with the paint brush and seeing what happened. You can judge for yourself what happened – it's different! But I think the painting creates the impression I *felt* so much at the time – that of a cold, silent, grey whiteness, relieved only by the brickwork of the cottages and the prominent chimneys.

I still don't know how I managed to sit in that snow-covered field and paint this picture without all my fingers freezing off, but somehow I lasted long enough to do the important bits – *and* before the gentlemen of the press arrived, whose presence has now become another anti-painting hazard!

9

WINTER SCENE

Sandringham, Norfolk 1987

This is one of my favourite sketches because I think I got the winter colours right and because the whole scene reminds me so much of a part of Norfolk I know and love with a passion. The great thing about painting snow scenes is that you can leave a lot of the page white and only fill in the really important bits. In this case the secret was to get the different tones right, but as far as I am concerned that is a hit or miss business!

In this sketch we are looking towards Sandringham House in the distance and I seem to recall that by now I had given up the unequal struggle and had anchored myself firmly to the car in order to avoid frostbite while in the pursuit of artistic verisimilitude! My whole year was made in 1990 when I discovered that my Prince's Trust had decided to use this sketch for their Christmas card last year. At least it had a 'Christmas look' about it!

c.'87

10

SHERNBORNE FIELD BARN

Norfolk 1991

This range of cottages and old cattle buildings sit well in the Norfolk landscape and have always been old favourites of mine. On this particular afternoon in January the light suddenly became utterly memorable — a phenomenon you might easily miss if painting didn't give you the excuse to remain in one spot for a decent length of time. I laboured to achieve the effect of the light because it was extraordinarily dramatic — especially with that spectacular cloud in the background. Norfolk is famed for the grandeur of its sky and this one lived up to a well-deserved reputation.

One of the greatest Norfolk artists who ever lived, and whom I was so privileged to know when I was young, Ted Seago, was a positive genius at capturing these sweeping East Anglian skies. But then he had studied meteorology, he told me, in minute detail and knew intimately each cloud type and formation. True artistry, I believe, is only possible when it involves intense study, constant application and years of practice. Those who take short cuts, or who claim that the kind of hard work necessary to learn the 'grammar' of drawing or painting is not necessary in the modern context are, I maintain, giving art a bad name.

11

WINDMILL AT BIRCHAM

Norfolk 1991

When I was a child this windmill had degenerated into a truncated stump, abandoned and sail-less. But in the last ten years, following its purchase by a talented enthusiast, it has been lovingly restored to its former glory. The owner scoured the countryside for authentic pieces of machinery and remade many of the fixtures. For me, the real joy was when the sails were replaced and the mill's white 'hat' once more enhanced the Norfolk skyline. After an interval of many years the windmill is grinding corn once again and giving constant pleasure to a succession of visitors.

It also gives great pleasure to *me* as it provides a wonderful focal point from many angles. I have immense admiration for the man who restored this windmill. Thank goodness someone minds enough to take such infinite trouble with these buildings which are such integral parts of the countryside.

12

VIEW OF WENSLEYDALE FROM MOORCOCK

North Yorkshire 1989

This part of the Yorkshire Dales is, without doubt, a very special piece of England. It is, in my humble opinion, one of the best examples of God and Man working in partnership over a long period of time to produce something organic and deeply satisfying. Everything seems to 'fit' in some extraordinary way. The undulating countryside invokes a natural rhythm that is almost tangible. The way in which the sky meets the horizon creates a natural harmony that is impossible to resist if you happen to be armed with a few brushes and some watercolour paints.

I'm afraid I haven't been very clever with this sketch. Maybe it's *partly* because it was getting very dark very quickly, and I was sitting on a grass slope amongst a large quantity of sheep droppings with my back beginning to give out and with pins and needles in my bottom...!

13

WENSLEYDALE

North Yorkshire 1989

This, I fear, is another very rapid sketch. I was out for a walk while staying briefly in the area and as I topped the skyline I suddenly came across this dramatic vista. It was altogether irresistible, so I very soon found myself installed in a damp patch of moorland grass trying to capture the atmosphere of the moment before the sun departed the scene and those expressive shadows vanished.

For the courageous reader who has managed to get this far in the book I would point out that this sketch is of the same valley as in the sketch on the previous page. Moorcock is down at the bottom left hand corner of this painting, at the foot of the hill. I would also point out that as a result of this sketch being reproduced in an article in a British Sunday newspaper's colour supplement, an art publishing company liked it so much that they asked if it could be made into a limited edition of lithographs. The same applied to the painting on the previous page.

14

VIEW OF PEEL HARBOUR FROM HMY BRITANNIA

Isle of Man 1989

I am afraid this is very much a miniature sketch which will require the use of a magnifying glass in order to see it. I will explain the reason for this.... I was on board the Royal Yacht *Britannia* when she anchored off this harbour in the Isle of Man in order that my parents could go ashore to carry out some engagements. I was much taken by the view when I emerged on deck after breakfast and decided that a sketch was necessary. The size of the sketch was dictated by the reality that we were anchored some way off shore, but the whole exercise was immensely complicated by the fact that no sooner had I started to draw the scene than the yacht weighed anchor and moved off to another part of the island. The frustration was intense, but there was nothing I could do about it because otherwise my parents would have been left standing on the jetty later in the day with no yacht in sight!

Hence I fear this sketch looks *exactly* as though it has been painted through the wrong end of a telescope while strapped to a moving object!

15

COUNTRYSIDE AROUND ABBEYSTEAD

Lancashire 1988

This was an extremely wet day, as you may be able to deduce from the rather soggy look of the finished product! Rather like the Yorkshire Dales, this country is wonderfully paintable. It is extraordinary how certain parts of the country cry out to be painted; you cannot ignore them without feeling in some way ungallant. There are other parts which leave me absolutely unmoved. They seem to have absolutely no character, or they are in areas where nearly all the trees have been removed and the hedges uprooted in a misguided attempt to maximize the yields from agricultural activity. Such places have had their souls torn out of them. They are sad, desolate, isolated places and they need the artist's touch to bring them back to life again.

I think you can see here, in this sketch, the way in which individual trees, hedges and woods give form and meaning to a landscape unless, that is, you are looking at something like a natural marsh, in which case the atmosphere is different and the trees form a distant backdrop.

This piece of country has a timeless quality about it and is gloriously 'English'.

JANUARY LANDSCAPE

Balmoral 1991

Try drawing Balmoral Castle – at any time of the year – and it will doubtless drive you mad with all its turrets, towers, pepperpots and embellishments! Having started this sketch I began to wonder what I had taken on. I found myself drawing the castle on a very small scale (I prefer this size of paper) which meant that I had to peer in an increasingly myopic fashion at what I was doing in order to get the proportions right.

In the foreground, where the shadows are, lies the cricket pitch where I used to play cricket in the school holidays with neighbouring schoolboys. Cricket was never my strong point and I would invariably walk boldly out to the crease only to return, ignominiously, a few minutes later when I was out for a duck. All the practice beforehand with my father and a friend from school was to no avail. That's why I took up polo! At least you stay out on the polo field for

the entire game and don't miss all the fun by being incarcerated in a pavilion.

VIEWS OF BALMORAL CASTLE

Balmoral 1989 & from Monaltrie 1990

I think I was completely mad to try the painting on the left, but it was the kind of challenge I could no longer resist. One thing I *have* discovered in the course of my fumbling painting efforts is that Balmoral Castle is marginally easier to paint than Sandringham House. Both seem to be peppered with turrets of various kinds and to boast the most complicated sorts of gables which defy my limited reserves of patience! But what I love about Balmoral, and this sketch was done in August, is the wonderful shadows. They, alone, made my painting finger itch, so I sat out in a field on three consecutive days at exactly the same time of day, being examined by some rather inquisitive Highland cows. This was my first attempt at drawing and painting the castle and I'm afraid it really isn't very good. The painting on the right is one of my favourite views of the castle as it rises majestically out of the encircling trees.

It is extraordinary to think that Prince Albert had a very considerable hand in the design of this castle which replaced a smaller house that was there when he and Queen Victoria first bought the estate. It was entirely built from granite quarried near the castle and, as far as I am concerned, is one of the most heavenly places on earth.

19

LOOKING TOWARDS DUBH LOCH

Balmoral 1989

This is one of those definitely unfinished sketches which went wrong in the right way! It *sometimes* happens, but not often. Half way through painting this view it started to rain, as you can see from the 'interesting' blotches all over the paper, and I was forced to abandon the rest of it. As it was in October the hillside had, in fact, taken on a remarkable orange glow in the afternoon sun, so what you see is *just* believable! I was intending to lay on several more washes and to put more shadow on the left-hand slope in the foreground, not to mention all the birches and rowans that need to go in, but nature intervened and when I got home I had to read to the children and ran out of time to finish this off!

In order to do this sketch I had to sit on a very steep slope above a loch. I hadn't been there long before I was somewhat startled by a very loud roar from a stag that was rounding up a party of hinds just below me. They had no idea I was in the vicinity because of the slope and because the wind was in my favour. Amidst a great deal of roaring and grunting the stag suddenly chased a hind right up to where I was sitting with a brush poised in my hand and a surprised look on my face. The surprised look on my face was nothing to the expression on the faces of the stag and hind when they saw me!

20

VIEW TOWARDS SANDY LOCH FROM BRIG O'DEE

Dee Valley 1988

For me, one of the most precious, and almost sacred, parts of the countryside around Balmoral is an area of ancient woodland which forms one of the few remnants of the great Caledonian forest that used to cover much of the Highlands. The fact that this part of it still exists at Balmoral is entirely due to the intervention of my great-great-great grandmother, Queen Victoria. The story goes that she was driving through this forest in her carriage shortly after she had bought the area in question from a neighbouring landowner. Hearing the sound of axes chopping wood in the distance, she stopped the carriage and sent someone to find out what was going on. The answer came back that the man from whom she had bought the forest had ordered the trees to be felled and sold. Outraged, she prohibited any more felling and immediately enquired of the neighbouring laird as to what he thought he was doing chopping down trees on her estate. His immediate response was that he had sold her the land, but not the trees! Queen Victoria duly had to buy the trees as well, and thank goodness she did....

21

ALLT-NA-GIUBHSAICH LODGE

Balmoral 1988

This was one of the small houses at Balmoral which Queen Victoria used to visit on some of her expeditions around that part of the country. On one occasion, she recounts in her journal, she was returning in her carriage from Allt-na-Giubhsaich (pronounced Alt-na-Gewsick!), accompanied by one of her daughters, when the wheel of the carriage struck a stone or the edge of the road and it promptly rolled over, tipping both occupants into the heather beside the road. Being made of stern stuff, the Queen quickly recovered her poise and waited happily by the side of the road till another carriage could be fetched to collect her. The moral of this story is that carriage-driving can be equally as dangerous as playing polo…!

As far as this sketch is concerned, you can see that I have chosen a pretty impossible angle from which to paint the house! It was a good, practical lesson in perspective, if nothing else.

22

ALLT-NA-GIUBHSAICH

Balmoral 1985

These cottages at Allt-na-Giubhsaich feature frequently in Queen Victoria's journal and, at some stage during my great-great-great grandmother's time, somebody must have laid out a rather nice garden in the foreground. You can see the remains of the 'bones' of it in the form of the Irish yews and the clumps of rhododendrons (even though they may not be recognizable in my sketch as I haven't yet fathomed out how to paint those bushes!) in front of the house. The garden has long since ceased to exist, the rhododendrons have gone wild and multiplied, and the rabbits have taken over the job as lawn-mowers.

Nowadays there is a constant stream of people passing by the cottages on their way to climb Lochnagar, which lies out of the picture to the left, and to return having groped their way through the mist or having twisted their ankles in unsuitable shoes.... It is wonderful that they all love and appreciate the grandeur of the wildness of this country, and the way in which these cottages complement so succinctly the immediate surroundings, as much as I do. What I *cannot* understand is why so many people should then show such scant regard for other travellers, and for the area as a whole, by mindlessly scattering rubbish wherever they go....

You would be appalled by how much there is.

23

LOCHNAGAR FROM INVERCAULD PARK

Dee Valley 1989

I suppose anyone who tries to paint has a favourite sketch of which they are particularly proud. This is mine. You may not believe it, but it *really* did look like this! It was one of those cold, grey and increasingly gloomy afternoons which often occur in April in the Highlands. It was all the more noticeable for having been rather a beautiful morning and I set out to paint after lunch full of optimism. As it turned out, I was presented with a much more interesting challenge to capture the mood of the occasion than if it had been peaceful sunshine.

The park at Invercauld, which lies further up the Dee Valley from Balmoral, is one of my favourite spots on Deeside. It was reputedly one of the first parks to be laid out in Scotland in the eighteenth century. The great clumps of 200-year-old larches were definitely sited by someone with an artist's eye and with a sensitive regard for that combination of nature's work and man's artifice which so characterized the incomparable legacy of our eighteenth-century forbears. To complete the romantic atmosphere of this ensemble of parkland, woods and mountains, the River Dee meanders gently through the whole scene before plummeting more violently beneath the Brig O'Dee.

24

LOCHNAGAR

Balmoral 1990

'*Years have roll'd on, Loch na Garr, since I left you. Years must elapse ere I tread you again: Nature of verdure and flowers has bereft you, Yet still are you dearer than Albion's Plain. England! thy beauties are tamed and domestic To one who has roved on the mountains afar: Oh for the crags that are wild and majestic! The steep frowning glories of dark Loch na Garr!*'

Thus wrote Lord Byron of the mountain that dominates the immediate surroundings of Balmoral. On his mother's side he was descended from the Gordons, many of whom fought for Bonnie Prince Charlie, and Balmoral is very much in Gordon country. In fact, Queen Victoria and Prince Albert bought Balmoral from a branch of the Gordon family. In his notes to the poem Lord Byron wrote that 'the most sublime feature of Lochin y Gair consists in those immense perpendicular cliffs of granite which give such impressive grandeur to its Northern Eastern aspect.'

The 'cliffs of granite', so beloved of generations of climbers, look delightfully harmless and tranquil in this sunset sketch. A patch of the mountain was illuminated in a golden, soothing light, but at any moment the scene could change:

'*Round Loch na Garr while the stormy mist gathers, Winter presides in his cold icy car: Clouds there encircle the forms of my fathers; They dwell in the tempests of dark Loch na Garr.*'

25 & 26

VIEWS OF LOCHNAGAR

From Balmoral 1989, & from Auchtavan 1990

As you thumb through the Scottish section of this book you will no doubt notice that Lochnagar features fairly frequently. This, I suppose, is hardly surprising as the mountain completely dominates the surrounding area and it looks different from every angle. Like all mountains it has a variety of moods. On the October day when I painted the view on the left it was looking delightfully benign, bathed in sparkling autumnal sunshine and dappled by the shadows cast by scudding clouds. But at other times it becomes fierce and brooding, even sinister on occasions. It is a mountain that needs to be treated with great respect, as a growing number of people have learnt to their cost.

Lochnagar features often in Queen Victoria's journal of her life in the Highlands. She and Prince Albert climbed it on several occasions, but principally with the assistance of a hill pony or two, if resident artists like Sir Edwin Landseer or the great watercolourist, Carl Haag, can be believed! These two remarkable painters stayed at Balmoral. Landseer's pastel pictures are justly famous, but Carl Haag is, I think, less well-known. His exquisite watercolour records of Queen Victoria's expeditions through the Highlands are amongst some of my most favourite pictures in the Royal Collection.

27

ALLT-NA-GIUBHSAICH, LOCHNAGAR BEYOND

Balmoral 1991

No, this is not unfinished this time! It is, believe it or not, a snow scene. As far as I am concerned, there is something infinitely enjoyable about painting things in the snow. The shadows take on a blueness that has a quality all of its own, and you are, in effect, painting only shadow in order to produce the desired effect.

I was lucky that the sun stayed out long enough for me to do this sketch, as it went in shortly afterwards and I never saw it again!

C'91

28

VIEW TOWARDS LOCHNAGAR

Balmoral 1988

I fear this is a very rough sketch, and yet *another* view of a distant Lochnagar fron a different angle! In the glen below are the remnants of what must have been a very extensive birch forest. Such birch forests clothed the glens and foothills of huge areas of the Highlands until the latter part of the nineteenth and the early twentieth century, when forestry plantations began to spread, and increased numbers of deer and sheep inhibited natural regeneration. To me, these remaining birch woods have an enthralling magic all of their own. Forget the English birch woods, they simply don't measure up to the weather-beaten, lichen-covered, gnarled grandeur of the Scottish ones…! When the sun is out and after it has rained, the tiny, delicate leaves sparkle like a thousand diamonds in the breeze. The shadows dancing under the trees and playing over the mossy grass and rocks create an Elysian atmosphere that strikes some primordial chord deep in one's heart. I only wish I could paint birch trees with any degree of success, but I haven't yet mastered the technique!

29 & 30

VIEWS OF BEN AVON

Balmoral 1990

I rather hope that the sketch on the left will prove to be an evocative one for those who know and love Scotland. The wind had gone into the North East and had cruelly extinguished the faint, but hopeful, traces of spring on the previous April day. Winter, lurking in the wings, had returned to the stage. The distant Cairngorms, the previous day so clear, benevolent and inviting in the sun, had now adopted an almost menacing and hostile guise in the strange yellow-grey light. It so clearly demonstrated the irresistible paradox of these mountains and, indeed, the giant paradox of Nature Herself which is reflected over and over again in ourselves. Everything has its opposite within it. Every advantage has a disadvantage, every success a failure. The secret it seems to me is to be aware and to attempt a reconciliation.

The sketch on the right shows yet another mood that passes over the countenance of these mountains. There is constant change, yet everything remains unaltered. The sense of timelessness is ever present and yet there is always, somewhere, a reminder of the transitory nature of material existence. Is it an illusion? Which is more real — what I see or what I feel and experience in my heart...? The urge to paint comes from within. Are there echoes of mountain ranges, trees and rivers; of majestic wild places; of storm and calm, in my soul?

70

31

LOOKING TOWARDS THE SPITTAL OF GLEN MUICK

Inchnabobart 1990

Scudding clouds gilded with a sudden shaft of evening sun, their shadows racing over the peat hags below.... (Try not to get carried away, you fool, or you'll sound pretentious and people will write to the newspapers complaining that The Prince of Wales is unfit to occupy his position because of his use of English!)

I wanted to paint this scene because I love those two small woods and they looked, suddenly, rather appetizing in that moment of light. The old drove road to Glen Clova runs behind the wood in the foreground and snakes up the hill beyond it, disappearing over the skyline behind the shoulder that is in shadow. Countless feet, both human and animal, must have trodden that path in days gone by. What hardy, self-reliant people they must have been....

32

LOOKING TOWARDS LOCH MUICK

Inchnabobart 1990

Returning in the evening from a day on the hill, I couldn't help noticing how the light had become a pale, hazy yellow and impossibly romantic. It was too much for me! I stopped the car, whipped out my paint bag and, pestered by midges, worked as fast as I could before this very special moment vanished.

This sketch is one of my favourites because, when I am feeling decidedly gloomy and claustrophobic in London, it reminds me of where my heart is....

33

GLEN MUICK FROM THE SPITTAL OF GLEN MUICK

Inchnabobart 1990

The Spittal of Glen Muick must have been a remarkable place in the old days. Just out of the picture in the bottom left-hand corner there used to be a whole series of buildings and walled enclosures associated with the ancient drove road that wends its way over the hill and down to Glen Clova in the next county of Angus. In the days when people drove their cattle and sheep from the summer grazing areas in the north to the markets and the wintering grounds in the south of Scotland, and back again in the spring, the Spittal of Glen Muick acted as a resting-place for the drovers and their flocks and herds. There must have been some great characters in those days; real individuals who understood the wiles and whims of nature and who had been brought up in an unforgiving environment.

The Spittal of Glen Muick was also reputed to be a major entrepot in the illicit whisky business – in fact there was an illegal still in the distant trees in the sketch – so it must have been quite a place until the Excise men finally got to it and destroyed the local economy....

34

HOUSE

Sutherland 1988

This painting is of a favourite place in Sutherland which I have known and loved since I was a child. The house is situated amidst some of the most wild and majestic country Scotland can produce. It truly is 'God's country', and those people who have been born in it, who live and work in it help to make it what it is. If it is true that environment plays a part in shaping the characters of men, then this magnificent part of the British Isles has been responsible for producing some of the most remarkable people I know.

When not lashed by hurricanes or swathed in cloud this part of the world is enveloped by swarms of midges – a kind of tiny fly which provides exquisite torture for any human being that shows his face in the vicinity. When I sat down on the rain-sodden grass to paint this picture not only did it proceed to drizzle (hence the spotty trees in the background on the right), but whole squadrons of midges located my position and carried out a series of mass attacks in the hope that I would call off my painting and retreat to a more strategic situation...! Despite the provocation I held my ground, finished the picture and staggered back to the house covered in little red spots! Such are the hazards of painting on the west coast of Scotland....

35

VIEW OF THE DEE VALLEY AND INVERCAULD

Ballochbuie Forest 1988

This sketch was done on a small writing card because, at the time, I was going through a phase of painting very small. This phase didn't last long and I soon reverted to a larger size of sketch pad. An interest in painting seems to encourage such phases or bouts of experimentation, but not all of them are successful by any means!

I am particularly fond of this view of the Dee Valley because of the way in which the organized planting of clumps of larches and pines in the park at Invercauld (at the bottom of the picture) provides such movement and interest for the eye. When the sun is out, which it invariably isn't by the time I reach my painting spot, the shadows cast by the clumps of trees add an even greater depth and fascination to the scene. In the background – much further away than you would think – the ground rises steeply and uncompromisingly to a series of great corries on Beinn A Bhuird and thence to the central massif of the Cairngorms. I remember flying a helicopter over the Cairngorms several years ago on a warm day in June or July and being astonished to see an entire herd of reindeer huddled together on the only remaining patch of snow on the very top of Cairngorm itself! I later recalled that there was indeed a herd of reindeer in that area, but they looked so incongruous when I was expecting red deer!

36

VIEW DOWN THE DEE VALLEY TOWARDS BALMORAL

Invercauld Castle 1988

This, believe it or not, is the same view as on page 61, but it was done in August or September as opposed to April. The whole mood is totally different. Everything looked softer, hazier and warmer, and my fingers didn't get so horribly cold!

I seem to recall that an artist I know asked if she could put this sketch into an exhibition she was organizing in London. Amazed, I said 'yes, of course', and thought nothing more of it. A few months later I was at a reception at The Royal Academy in London when a lady came up to me saying she very much wanted to buy this painting, and an accompanying one, which she had seen at the exhibition. Apparently she had been round the exhibition and had particularly liked my sketches, but (and this is the best part, as far as I'm concerned!) she didn't know they were by me. Upon being told that I had painted them she was rather annoyed and vowed to track me down! I still haven't sold them to her – I wouldn't know what price to put on them!

37

LOOKING TOWARDS MAR LODGE IN THE RAIN

Dee Valley 1988

This view up the Dee Valley, from a particular spot which I love, is one of the most dramatic and majestic on Deeside. I return to it as often as I can because it is always different. The light is never the same. The hills are constantly altering their appearance in this changing light and when the lengthening shadows come in the evening the whole effect takes your breath away. One minute, as in this almost ruinously 'moist' sketch (which I had to abandon because a huge shower overcame me!), the whole valley becomes blurred, mysterious and saturated, the next it is bathed in an ethereal silver light which picks out the meandering river as if it was a sparkling ribbon cast down from a present in heaven.

The wonderful thing about painting is that it provides you with an excuse to sit in one spot long enough to appreciate the quality of the changing light and the theatrical effects of the weather on the landscape. Turner was one of the great geniuses of English art who understood this so well and whose sketches and paintings betray this deep and unstoppable passion for the beauty of God's creation. I only wish I could have been lucky enough to have had a few lessons from such a man, but the chances are I would merely have become insanely frustrated and given up in despair!

38

COTTAGE

Invercauld 1989

If you are looking at the view on page 61 and then you turn around and look up the Dee Valley from the same spot you will see this view. Upstream from here lies Mar Lodge estate with its vast and incongruous, suburban-looking Swiss Cottage-style of a house. Anything, you would think, less appropriate for that setting would be hard to find, which is why I haven't been able to bring myself to try to paint it! But, nevertheless, it was built for one of Queen Victoria's granddaughters who married The Duke of Fife and Queen Victoria often used to visit the place while at Balmoral.

The cottage in this sketch fits more suitably, and more picturesquely, into the landscape with those splendid old Scots pines providing a solid and reassuring backdrop. In the near distance birch trees clothe the hillside like stubble on a chin and beyond that are the snow-covered mountains of the Cairngorms. I have done better with the background in this picture, but have failed to do justice to the foreground. The river is unfinished and so is the cottage. I can only plead the fact that my fingers had frozen by the time I reached the foreground and a very nasty, wintry drizzle forced me to accept the fact that art, in this instance, had to give way to survival!

39

INVERCAULD AND THE DEE VALLEY

Ballochbuie Forest 1990

I have sketched this view on several occasions, and it is always a tempting one which draws me back over and over again. Apart from the tantalizing glimpses of the Dee as it meanders through the great park of Invercauld, it is the countless different tones of green of the trees which fascinate me.

Painting helps to make you aware of many details which you might otherwise miss. Have you noticed how intrusive, uncompromising and unnatural are the hard edges provided by the huge monocultural plantations of fir trees which we now see, grown like fields of wheat, all over the countryside? Why is it that we still persist in pursuing a clear-felling forestry policy, which involves combine-harvesting a crop of identical trees all grown in gigantic furrows ploughed through the peat by vast machines, rather than taking the long-term, far-sighted approach and adopting what is known as an 'uneven age group' system? This description is forester's jargon for a natural regeneration system of forestry which works *with* nature, not against it as in the monocultural plantations. The immovable, invariable, insufferable reason given for this state of affairs is, wait for it, 'cost effectiveness', 'efficiency' and 'economic necessity!' but which system is *ultimately* the more sustainable and sensible...?

40

THE DEE VALLEY

Invercauld 1990

This is another sketch of one of my favourite Deeside views, but in this particular case I completed it before it began to rain! There is a lot to paint in a view like this, so you need at least two hours without rain.... For some strange reason I find it extraordinarily hard, if I haven't finished a painting, to return on another day and to pick up where I left off. The atmosphere is never the same and the 'moment' has passed. Hence so many unfinished sketches!

41

BRIG O'DEE

Dee Valley 1989

I fear this is perhaps rather an obvious 'chocolate box' kind of sketch.... The old Brig O'Dee is one of the most famous landmarks on Deeside and marks the western extremity of the Balmoral estate. It was built during the aftermath of the 1752 uprising by engineers attached to Viscount Bury's troops and is, I think, a classic example of the art of eighteenth-century bridge construction. It also demonstrates how utterly appropriate the curve of an arch is; how much more natural and fitting it is than the uncompromising harshness of a straight line. Imagine a modern, single span, concrete bridge on the same site and the heart goes cold – or, at least, *mine* does! And yet this is what is happening all over Scotland, in so many of the most beautiful and unspoilt places. Whilst *some* bridges like the Brig O'Dee are renovated and retained for modern use, many other smaller ones of enormous character and charm are cut off like pathetic refugees and a new, character-less, municipal object that is repeated with monotonous regularity all over the Highlands is put in its place nearby. *Surely*, with all our modern technological ingenuity, you would think it would be possible to design contemporary bridges with arches made of concrete or, better still, to strengthen or widen the existing bridges so that they could take the traffic loads of today?

42

VIEW OVER THE DEE VALLEY LOOKING SOUTH

Corndavon 1990

I almost bit off more than I could chew with this sketch.... It took me far longer than I had intended and, as it was October, my fingers lost most of their feeling. Then the paint refused to dry on the paper and my patience began to fray at the edges! The final straw was when my two terriers vanished, having presumably become exasperated by my inability to move out of one spot.

The autumn colours were by now at their best and the Dee Valley was ablaze with orange, yellow, red and russet hues. They aren't easy to paint well, because it is only too easy to make them seem unreal if you aren't careful.

43

VIEW OF DORNOCH

Sutherland 1989

No sooner had I settled down to paint this scene on a beach on the northern shore of the Dornoch Firth in north-east Scotland than I saw a posse of press photographers, crouched in the sand dunes, pointing their ridiculously long lenses in my direction. On such occasions I try hard to ignore the intrusiveness of their photographic paraphernalia, but it makes it peculiarly difficult to concentrate when you know that every expression on your face, every movement or gesture you make is being magnified in close-up. Whether they use the photographs or not, your imagination plays on the predictable captions to accompany them… 'Beach Boy Charlie paints alone', or, better still, 'Beached Wales – the Paint-Potty Prince Revealed'!

C '89

44

CASTLE OF MEY

Caithness 1986

The Castle of Mey is one of those genuinely Scottish castles which stands on a rocky headland on the northern tip of Scotland. It is either battered by gales or swathed in a damp mist that rolls in from the Pentland Firth. Every now and then, as if by magic, the sun comes out and suddenly the fields become emerald green and the sea a sapphire blue. The scene is transformed into something peaceful and pastoral, but it is all very deceptive....

My grandmother came across this castle, then virtually a ruin, on a visit to Caithness some thirty to forty years ago. She fell in love with it, felt sorry for it and wanted to do something about it. Since then she has lovingly restored it, resurrected the old walled kitchen garden – the only place where anything will grow because of the shelter – and taken an enormous interest in all the local activities whenever she can. I painted this sketch during a short visit to my grandmother one August. I like to think that if I did the painting again today I would do it better. 1986 seems a long way away and I'm learning all the time!

On either side of the castle, as you can see in this picture, there are wonderful old woods of stunted sycamore which look exactly as though they have been brushed in one direction and then given a very good trim by some unseen barber.

98

CASTLE OF MEY
'86

San Gimignano

45

VIEW FROM VILLA LA FOCE

Near Montepulciano, Tuscany 1986

Invariably other people's ideas of what makes a good view to paint do not coincide with mine, so I need to search for myself until I find the ideal position. This often entails a great deal of walking to and fro and shifting of positions. A tree is in the way here, or a building there. Sometimes a posse of policemen is in the way! Having found a suitable spot, at last, the light invariably changes, or goes altogether. Despair! Muttering and oaths follow. The water jar gets knocked over in the hurry. More oaths, and policemen emerge from behind cypress trees to investigate the incantations!

In this case I was confronted by the extraordinary barren and empty landscape of Northern Tuscany. In some ways, it gives the appearance of having once been the site of endless china clay workings, with all the trees having been cut down and with a few bushes growing here and there. It seems the countryside has remained substantially unchanged since the days of those great artists of the thirteenth and fourteenth centuries who painted that landscape in their religious pictures which I had previously believed was purely imaginary. I chose *this* view because the zig-zag line of cypress trees lining the track up the hill provided an 'anchor' for the sketch. I didn't do it very well, but at least it reminds me of that day in my life and is full of happy associations.

View from Villa
La Foce, near
Montepulciano - Tuscany - April 1986

46

VIEW OF CACCHIANO FROM BROLIO

Tuscany 1987

This was an after-lunch sketch. When I had finally extracted myself from yet another delicious and memorable Italian lunch, and all the other guests had settled down for what I suspect was a siesta, I went off to explore the local area on foot. I glimpsed this gloriously evocative Tuscan view, having only gone a short distance, and settled down, if that is the right word, in the most strategic spot — which happened to be a rather knobbly ploughed field. Nearby, there was a hedge full of Buddleias, around which clouds of peacock butterflies were gathering as if they knew they had found the only pub for the next hundred miles!

The afternoon proved to be one of those rather sultry, leaden affairs where the light has a nasty tendency to go flat and uninteresting. However, I persevered because I loved that small village squatting on the skyline with the appetising lines of the terraces combed on to the hillside around it, and the oakwoods tumbling down the slope into the valley below. When this sketch was first published about two years ago, I received a letter from someone who had fought his way through this part of Italy during the last war while serving with the British Army. He had seen my sketch and had immediately recognized the area as being the site of an engagement with German forces. I was encouraged that my painting had been accurate enough to evoke this response!

BROLIO
TUSCANY

47

VIEW FROM IL CORNETO

Tuscany 1987

A warm morning in early May... Sir Harold Acton, that incomparable Anglo-Italian character and lover of all the arts of life, had recommended a visit to the house of an artist he knew. The view was breathtaking and receded into the tantalizing blue distance of the Tuscan hills. In order for me to have a chance of painting even moderately well I need to be inspired, and this great sweep of countryside with the group of buildings and inviting cypress trees in the foreground provided just what was necessary.

The trouble, as you can see from the unfinished nature of this sketch, was that the subject was too large for the time I had available. Just as I was really becoming immersed in the subject I had to tear myself away – literally – and the result is something of a challenge to the powers of imagination of the reader. But the recollection of that Elysian view is firmly etched upon my mind, with its patchwork of vineyards, olive groves and ploughed fields interspersed by rolling woods of stunted oak. The olive groves in the foreground gave the whole scene a reassuring, timeless quality. Don't you feel that olive trees themselves, with their gnarled and wisely ancient appearance, have an aspect of 'belonging', which in turn makes you feel that all is well with the world and with our place in the scheme of things?

106

C. 1987

48

VIEW FROM VILLA EMO

Near Padua 1987

I confess that this is a sketch of which I am rather proud. It was originally part of a slightly larger painting, but I cut it down rather ruthlessly on both sides because I was not so proud of what I had painted on the margins. The result, I think, has more substance and what I particularly liked was the shadow on the fountain in the foreground which helps to give the rest of the picture some depth.

For me, the sketch is quintessentially 'Italian' and I was thrilled to find that the organizers of my exhibition in Urbino in 1990 had chosen this picture for the poster advertising the exhibition in Raphael's house. It was an extraordinary feeling to walk through the streets of Urbino and to find my much enlarged sketch posted on to the walls of houses!

49

VILLA RIVELLA DE MONSELICE

Italy 1987

This is a house near Padua which was reputedly designed by one of Andrea Palladio's pupils, called Scamozzi. I fear I have not done Signor Scamozzi any justice by the way in which I have portrayed his architectural efforts, but that may be due to the fact that my sketching activities were curtailed by the necessity to prepare myself for dinner with forty people that evening, as much as it is due to untutored attempts to control a pencil.

It is only when you start to draw a building that you appreciate just how extraordinarily difficult it is to do it really well. The same is true for so many things in life that we haven't tried or experienced ourselves. The real experts or professionals make it look astonishingly easy and effortless. Not until you try it for yourself do you realize how much practice and dedication is involved. Nothing is truly worthwhile or of lasting value unless it has involved very considerable effort and application. Cutting corners and reducing the amount of effort may appear to be more 'cost-effective' and more 'progressive', but in the long run this will prove to be illusory.

50

NOTO

Sicily 1990

Noto is one of those rare towns in Sicily which has managed to escape some of the worst ravages of insensitive development and brutal planning. Although the centre of the town is crumbling fast and it bears all the signs of a faded former glory, it still has an enormous attraction and some very fine buildings.

On turning a corner in the road to Noto, this view of the town nestling between groves of olives and fruit trees suddenly presented itself. Although it was a town it seemed almost as if it was a natural feature of the countryside, such was its organic appearance. The moment I saw its situation I experienced that inexplicable feeling that it was 'right'; that it 'belonged', in some uncanny way, to its surroundings and that it complemented those surroundings rather than detracted from them.

Do you ever experience similar feelings when travelling at home or abroad and you come across a village, or a town, or a particular house that literally raises your spirits and makes you want to cry out in admiration and appreciation? If you do, then you will probably also realize that the characteristics which have excited your admiration do not happen purely by accident and that a great deal of thought and trouble were taken at the outset over the siting and design.

112

51

FARMHOUSE AT LES VARRIERES

Provence 1989

Next to Italy, Provence holds a rather special allure for me. Maybe it is partly because in times gone by Provence used to be a part of Italy and, at one point, the popes were even resident in Avignon. The food, too, has Italian undertones and if you are like me you find that the whole of life is transformed into a new and aromatic experience by the way in which herbs of all kinds are used in the cooking.

Invariably, whenever I manage to go to Provence, the weather does something which all the locals assure me it has never done before. It is almost as if Murphy's Law had been defined entirely as a result of my experience. Wherever I go in the world I am always told that I should have been there yesterday! In Provence you are supposed to find permanently blue, Cezanne-like skies with matching Impressionist shadows. In my case I am greeted by leaden clouds and tropical downpours…. When I stopped to do this sketch of an abandoned farmhouse the Cezanne conditions had been re-established. On the right of the buildings there was a very beautiful oak copse, beyond which the ground dropped away to a spectacular view over the receding plain. The whole scene conveyed an atmosphere of remote tranquillity which inspired me to try and translate that atmosphere on to paper.

VIEW FROM SEGURET TOWARDS AVIGNON

Provence 1989

This horribly unfinished and hasty sketch was the result of being taken to see one of those Provençal villages which seemed to have been carved out of the side of a hill. I fell a hopeless victim to the tantalizing view and then promptly ran out of time because darkness fell! The 'organic' growth of the village gave you the impression that it truly *belonged* to the hillside, rather than having been thrust upon it. For all I know, as with one or two Provençal villages I have come across, most of the houses may have been owned by eminent architects...!

I often ask myself what it is about certain landscapes, or certain views, which makes me so eager to paint them. This one just *had* to be painted. There are plenty of views which have no effect on me whatsoever, but why *is* this? I can only assume, and you must forgive me for groping for the best way in which to describe this curious phenomenon, that certain ones strike a chord with some inner landscape of the mind. And yet the pure *feeling* that is thus engendered is actually experienced in the heart, as I am sure many people will recognize who have a similar feeling when confronted by something of beauty and harmony. The sensation is almost the same as that produced by music and is deeply reassuring.

c.89

c '89
FROM GEGURET
TOWARDS AVIGNON

53 & 54

VIEWS OF VALLDEMOSA

Majorca 1986

This village in Majorca is one of the most attractive on the island. If you approach it from the valley below, at a time when the evening sun bathes it in a golden light and daubs long shadows across the buildings and out into the surrounding olive groves, you suddenly find yourself begging to stop the car in order to appreciate it the better.

I can only say that I had immense problems trying to find a suitable place from which to paint the view on the left. After much trial and error the only place I could find obliged me to sit on a crumbling stone wall in an olive grove which merely had a devastating and paralysing effect upon my posterior! When I finally arose from this excruciating position, as it became too dark to see what I was doing, my legs failed to function properly and I fell down the terrace into the olive grove below.

The sketch on the right is of the other side of Valldemosa done on the following evening. Somewhere near the church in this painting is the house that the composer, Frédéric Chopin, used to inhabit when he came to the village in the last century. I like to think of him finding renewed inspiration in this sun-swept environment where the pace of life tends to match the natural rhythms of the earth.

VILLAGE

Majorca 1990

Personally, I am not very proud of this sketch, but when it was seen by one or two artists whom I know they said it ought to be included in this book. I respect their judgement! It was the first sketch I tried to do with my right hand after I had carelessly broken my arm in two places. The day before I had tried painting with my left hand because my right arm was in a sling and I didn't think I would be able to paint right-handed. Such was the messy disaster brought about by my 'sinister' efforts that I resolved to experiment with my other hand the next day.

By holding the sketch pad in my left hand and bringing it as near to my chest as possible I was able to use a pencil and paintbrush in my right hand and to produce this untidy sketch of part of a Majorcan hill village. The light was virtually impossible, as by that time in the evening I was looking into a hazy sun and could hardly make out the buildings. It was also the first time I had picked up a brush for three months, so I was doubly handicapped!

56

ANDRAITX HARBOUR

Majorca 1988

Andraitx is another of the rather more attractive small towns in Majorca with a busy harbour full of yachts and general tourist activity. Trying to find a quiet spot in the evening from which to paint this view was quite impossible. Abandoning all hope, I walked out to the end of a long breakwater in the harbour and settled myself beneath a small lighthouse. No sooner had I begun to sketch in the outline of this view than the first of a succession of people out for an evening stroll along the jetty leant over my shoulder to peer at what I was doing and to ask a series of surprisingly obvious questions. As many of them seemed to be British tourists the situation became increasingly interesting! Under the circumstances it became harder and harder to concentrate properly on what I was doing. It also grew darker rather sooner than I had expected, so the combination of events ensured a less than satisfactory result. The boats seem to be set fast in a pale blue concrete, rather than an enticing piece of the Mediterranean, and half the houses that *should* have been in the picture have mysteriously de-materialized.... But the great thing is that it couldn't possibly be mistaken for Bognor Regis!

57

FARMHOUSE

Majorca 1990

This scene is wonderfully evocative to me of warm August evenings in Majorca; of Mediterranean smells and sheep bells; of olive groves; cypress trees and honey-coloured farm buildings. It is a frozen memory in the diary of my life; a mere blink in time, but full of happy recollections. In the background I could hear police radios crackling. The Spanish police were probably checking them to see why they were still working!

I liked the orange cliff in the distance and the way in which the setting sun made it even more complementary to the farm buildings beside it. I loved the shadows on the buildings....

Oh, help! Look at the time – I shall be late for dinner again!

58

FARMHOUSE

Majorca 1990

I spotted this enticing view during a search for paintable scenes in Majorca. Having found it, we had to go on in the car until we could find a place to turn around and return to the best spot from which to paint. As it was in August there were terrible scenes with coaches and their irritated drivers. Meanwhile, I did my best to disguise myself by burying my head in the sling supporting my injured arm and pretending I wasn't there! At length I found a position beside an ancient, knobbly olive tree while the policemen settled down to soak up the last rays of the evening sun and presumably to discuss the next person who might help them with their enquiries....

I was enormously taken with this farm and with its beautiful situation. When I arrived the sun was shining like a searchlight over the rim of the steep hills to the right and picking out the trees around the farmhouse, while the hill in the background was increasingly in deeper shadow, adding to the wonderful contrast. The serrated cypress trees at the foot of the hill gave the whole scene an eccentric charm, but what made it for me was the elegant chance of that single cypress at the right-hand end of the farmhouse.

59

FARMHOUSE

Majorca 1990

This building caught my eye on an evening painting expedition. By the time I had made up my mind to try to paint it, having rejected other less satisfactory alternatives, the sun was very nearly below the horizon. I just had time to see it bathe the western walls of the house in an orange-pink hue before it slipped from sight and I was left with a series of increasingly indistinct shapes in the twilight.

Painting in the dark is a novel pastime, but not recommended, because when you return to the light you invariably discover that the colours you have used are far too pale and insignificant. In this case I was just back to my old tricks of failing to finish anything!

IMAGES FROM FURTHER AFIELD

60

BODRUM CASTLE

Turkey 1989

When I first showed this painting to one or two people they thought it was of Windsor Castle – by the sea! In fact it is in the Eastern Mediterranean on one of the last relatively unspoilt stretches of coastline in Turkey. So much of the Mediterranean coast has already been destroyed beyond recognition by totally insensitive development and a lack of long-term planning that I hardly dare to imagine what will happen to this area in the next few years. It would be worse than a tragedy if this ancient and historic part of Asia Minor, a crossroads for all the greatest civilizations the Western world has seen, was to be disfigured for ever by the acne of third-rate development and general shoddiness.

As a former fortress of the Knights of St John, Bodrum Castle guards the seaward side of the town known to the ancient world as Halicarnassus. I have employed a considerable degree of artistic licence in this picture because the whole of the foreground was, in fact, clogged with boats of every shape and size, while immediately below me the promenade was equally clogged with large numbers of very puce-coloured British tourists of varying dimensions....

C. '89

61 & 62

VIEWS OF FETHIYE

Turkey 1989

In the view on the left I was finding it quite difficult to discover anything suitable to paint. There was nothing obvious and it was becoming rather hot. The light was growing more harsh as the day advanced, and the shadows were shrinking. I decided to give myself something difficult to paint in just a piece of sloping Turkey on a hot day. The result looks much better if you put it against the back of a chair and look at it through a pair of binoculars from a considerable distance....

If you were looking at the view on the left and then turned through 180° your attention would have been arrested by the distant mountain-scape in the painting on the right. I got up at five o'clock in the morning to capture the scene and was overwhelmed by the palpable and almost 'painful' beauty of this sunrise. My mind wandered from the task in hand.... Surely this was the same sky, the same violet light, the same rolling hills as met the gaze of the great heroes of classical times? There was nothing to have altered this timeless scene. Somehow the knowledge was unutterably reassuring and helped to place my own transitory existence in proportion.

134

YASICILAR ISLANDS
FETHIYE BAY.

63

VIEW FROM PRIENE

Turkey 1989

All over Eastern Turkey there are the remains of some remarkable Hellenistic towns. Priene is one of them. It is situated on a rocky hill rising out of a flat plain and was constructed on a well-planned grid pattern. You approach it by what must originally have been a very fine stone-flagged street and after puffing your way up the hill you arrive, glistening with perspiration and surrounded by people wearing funny sun-hats and Japanese cameras, at the site of the collapsed temple. All around are piles of the original stones and the recumbent shapes of what remains of Doric, Ionic and Corinthian columns.

Having examined the ruins from every possible angle, I came to the conclusion that to try to paint them would inevitably end in tears, so I retreated to the edge of the site overlooking the hot, dusty plain and the shimmering distance beyond. I was determined to try and capture that overwhelming feeling of distance. The gradually receding clumps of cypress trees make wonderful reference points and help to hold the painting together. Fenland farmers who may regard this sketch could be forgiven for wondering if the view might be of Cambridgeshire during a particularly hot summer...!

C. '88

64

SUNSET IN THE MEDITERRANEAN

Turkey 1989

Rarely have I witnessed a more romantic sunset than this one in the eastern Mediterranean. Trying to capture its transitory translucence was beyond me, as you can see from this rather 'agricultural' sketch, but the desire to get out my paint box and to crouch amongst the painful rocks of a Turkish island was overwhelming.

The trouble with sunsets, or sunrises, is deciding at what rapidly changing point to close, as it were, the aperture of the mind so that you imprint on your memory a particular moment in the kaleidoscopic display of colour effects that is taking place. If I was as clever and observant as Monet, I would take notes at frequent intervals and then produce about ten paintings of the same scene at different moments. But I'm *not*, which is only too obvious!

65

HMY BRITANNIA AND ESCORT AT ANCHOR

Double Haven Bay, Hong Kong 1989

During an official visit to Hong Kong I had a day off in HMY *Britannia* and she anchored in this rather lovely bay in the New Territories. It was a thoroughly restorative contrast to all my other activities to be able to go ashore on a small island with a sandwich in my paint bag and to find a gap in some very prickly bushes from which to make this sketch. As the sun went down, everything turned a pale violet colour (including, by this time, the bruises on my bottom...!) and the two ships at anchor made rather a good subject.

Painting ships requires practice, and I haven't had enough of it.... On top of that, something rather nasty and brown seems to have seeped out of a leaking bottle in my paint bag and spread a sepia tinge along the shoreline and half way up the hills on the far side of the bay. I can only apologise for this and claim the excuse that it happened when I jumped down into the boat off the jetty!

66

VIEW OF THE BAY FROM HMY BRITANNIA

Double Haven Bay, Hong Kong 1989

I rather feel that this painting should be entitled 'Farewell to Empire' or 'Poor *Britannia!*'. Having been brought up with the Royal Navy in my blood – both my great-grandfathers, my grandfather, my great uncle and my father all served in it – and having spent a considerable time on board the Royal Yacht *Britannia* at the age of five, before serving in the RN myself – the White Ensign has a peculiarly romantic association for me. To some, in the past, I dare say it struck fear into their hearts. To others, it must have symbolized hope, release from slavery and oppression, the protection of fragile democratic rights or the freedom to go about their lawful business upon the seas. To me, it is a potent symbol of those high standards to which the Royal Navy still adheres in a world where such standards are increasingly difficult to maintain.

The White Ensign is also rather enjoyable to paint, even if it never stops flapping about and is impossible to capture in one position. On this occasion there was a beautiful sunset over the distant Chinese hills and the White Ensign was flapping gently to and fro in the soft breeze. The whole scene was gloriously peaceful and I found it impossible to resist the urge to capture this atmosphere.

67

VIEW OF DESERT

Oman 1986

During a day off in the middle of an official tour of Gulf countries I managed to explore a remote corner of Oman, where I found this view. Nearby was a small fishing village with a group of men and young boys sitting in the shade of a large tree and discussing, no doubt, questions of philosophical importance.... Not a single woman in sight. Our appearance created a certain amount of interest amongst the 'Shady Tree' crowd, but I slunk off to settle myself into what I hoped was a relatively scorpion-free zone in order to create this Middle Eastern Masterpiece. The colours in that part of the world can be breathtaking. You would think it was all yellow ochre sand, but in the early mornings and evenings the rocky outcrops momentarily become flushed with orange, pink, purple and violet. In these circumstances a good memory is incredibly helpful!

C. 1986
OMAN

68

PORT SUEZ

Egypt 1986

If you have ever been through the Suez Canal you will probably know that it is necessary to queue up at either end of the canal before the authorities permit you to enter. You then transit the canal as part of a pre-arranged batch of ships. It was while at anchor off Port Suez in HMY *Britannia* that I thought I would try my hand at maritime painting, and this is the rather uncertain result....

Painting ships, like dogs or children, can be extraordinarily frustrating because they have an unfortunate tendency to move all the time. Ships swing at anchor in a most aggravating fashion and the aspect changes at once. You then have to wait, with mounting impatience, for them to swing back again. On this particular occasion it was one of those hot, windless days when the sea became like a mirror and the shore in the background seemed to evaporate into a shimmering, khaki-magenta haze. Here and there becalmed Egyptian sailing boats floated about like spent mayflies on an English chalk stream. At any moment one expected them to be devoured by some enormous trout. Looking at this sketch brings all the sights, sounds and smells of that Middle Eastern day flooding back again as if it were yesterday.

69

ALDIR'IYAH VILLAGE

Saudi Arabia 1989

This sketch was the result of one of those hastily-grabbed moments during the course of a rather official visit to this preserved, but abandoned, village not far from the capital city of Saudi Arabia, Riyadh. Most sensible people would have taken a few photographs but, being a stubborn sort of person, I persisted with my sketching activities.

There aren't many places like this left in Saudi Arabia (this one was only saved from ruin because it was at one point the home of the Al Saud family), owing to the fact that, in common with so many other countries experiencing rapid development, anything redolent of a former traditional existence is abandoned or destroyed in the rush to adopt the worst aspects of a Western, or American, model. So often people only discover what has been lost to their cultural heritage, and thus excised from their souls, too late. In Saudi Arabia's case there is, at last, a re-awakening of interest in Islamic culture and design; in building methods that may be more appropriate to the climatic conditions, and which lead to a more sustainable approach in the long term.

ALDIR'IYAH VILLAGE - SAUDI ARABIA   CW '89

70

DOHA

Qatar 1986

This was the view I had from my room in an official guest house in Doha, the capital city of the Gulf state of Qatar. It wasn't the most alluring view I had ever seen, but it was all I could find under the circumstances. The sun had set and the mosque in the background lent a certain degree of authenticity to this Arab scene. From the mosque came the amplified and recorded voice of the muezzin calling the faithful to prayer, something which you were pretty certain would be repeated at five o'clock the following morning...!

C. 1986 DOHA, QATAR

71

THE MONASTERY, PETRA

Jordan 1985

Petra, that ancient city carved out of rock in a Jordanian valley, has a magic that is entirely unique. When you see it you can only marvel, open-mouthed, at the sheer technical achievement involved in carving the most beautiful, classical facades out of the solid rock faces of a narrow valley. As if these facades were not enough, the ancient inhabitants of this city also sculpted an amphitheatre out of the hillside and hacked beautifully-made paths through the rocky terrain. In its heyday it must surely have been one of the wonders of the ancient world, in a region that was very much the cradle of Western civilization.

The building or, more accurately, the sculpted edifice, in this painting is known as The Monastery and can only be reached by a long climb up one of the stone paths through a rocky pass. Nearby the ground plunges thousands of feet into great jagged ravines. Bridges of rose-coloured and ochre rock overlap like waves as they recede into the hazy distance and nowhere is a single blade of grass or tree to be seen.

72

GABASADI ISLAND, NTWETWE PAN

Botswana 1987

This extraordinarily inhospitable part of the world is in the Kalahari desert in Botswana. The Ntwetwe Pan is one of the vast, dried-up, shallow lakes which formed in natural depressions in the surrounding desert and into which, whenever there is enough rainfall elsewhere in Africa, the Okavango River overflows. When this happens, all too rarely, flamingoes and wildlife of all sorts appear as if by magic to take advantage of the benefits provided by the water. When I travelled through this area on a four-day safari it was in the grip of a pretty fearsome drought and the hard white surface of the salt pan acted as a giant reflector to the relentless power of the sun.

Initially the area had seemed harsh and alien, but then I very quickly discovered that to describe the countryside as a desert gave an entirely false impression. It consisted chiefly of dry bush country, but as you moved across it so the vegetation changed, and there were even large areas covered in palm trees and thicker bush. The only *real* desert I found was where the over-stocking of cattle, or goats, had destroyed the vegetation in large areas around man-made boreholes. This, of course, is one of the most devastating and tragic disasters that threatens to overwhelm vast areas of Africa and to produce famine and death on a gigantic scale....

154

GABASADI ISLAND,
NTWETWE PAN,
KALAHARI, APRIL '87

73

NAABI HILL FROM LAKE LAGAJI

Serengeti Plain, Tanzania 1988

One of the most difficult things about painting in Africa, apart from the fact that the watercolour evaporates in the heat, is trying to convey the mirage effect which is so often present. I very quickly discovered that it is far better to paint in the early mornings or evenings (as, indeed, it is anywhere), but on this occasion I was mad enough to set myself the challenge of trying to capture the shimmering afternoon distance of the Serengeti Plain.

Propping myself against a red-hot Land Rover, I proved to my entire satisfaction that taking a photograph is infinitely easier, probably more economical, certainly less time-consuming and conceivably less injurious to your health if, by hanging around, you unwittingly become lion-bait, than fiddling about with paints. But it is so much less rewarding!

At the time I was in the Serengeti area the wildebeest and zebra migration was at its height. As far as the eye could see the plains were covered in vast herds of these animals — perhaps a million or more. In some uncanny way they could invariably tell where the rain had fallen in this immense sea of grass and wild flowers, and would head for where the grazing was best. Believe it or not, the distant dots you can see in my sketch are not trees or bushes, but simply *thousands* of wildebeest and zebra apparently floating above the horizon in the heat haze.

ENGLISH SCENES

1 WINDSOR CASTLE
Berkshire 1990 11.5 x 23.8 cm Page18

2 PRINCE ALBERT'S KITCHEN GARDEN BUILDINGS
Windsor 1989 12.1 x 27.0 cm Page 20

3 LOOKING TOWARDS NORTH CREAKE
Holkham, Norfolk 1990 15.2 x 24.5 cm Page 22

4 SANDRINGHAM HOUSE
Norfolk 1987 17 x 24.5 cm 1991 Page 24

5 VIEW OF HILLINGTON ON A JANUARY AFTERNOON
Norfolk 1990 15.0 x 22.5 cm Page 26

6 JANUARY SUNSET LOOKING TOWARDS HILLINGTON
Norfolk 1990 14.5 x 24.5 cm Page 26

7 FARM BUILDINGS
Norfolk 1987 8.8 x 9.5 cm Page 28

8 COTTAGES IN THE SNOW
Sandringham, Norfolk 1987 24.0 x 34.5 cm Page 30

9 WINTER SCENE
Sandringham, Norfolk 1987 13.1 x 22.5 cm Page 32

10 SHERNBORNE FIELD BARN
Norfolk 1991 17.3 x 24.7 cm Page 34

11 WINDMILL AT BIRCHAM
Norfolk 1991 17.0 x 24.5 cm Page 36 & Frontispiece

12 VIEW OF WENSLEYDALE FROM MOORCOCK
North Yorkshire 1989 16.1 x 25.6 cm Page 38

13 WENSLEYDALE
North Yorkshire 1989 11.5 x 17.0 cm Page 40

14 VIEW OF PEEL HARBOUR FROM HMY BRITANNIA
Isle of Man 1989 3.7 x 16.5 cm Page 42

15 COUNTRYSIDE AROUND ABBEYSTEAD
Lancashire 1988 12.1 x 17.4 cm Page 44

IMPRESSIONS OF SCOTLAND

16 JANUARY LANDSCAPE
Balmoral 1991 14.0 x 24.2 cm Page 48

17 VIEW OF THE CASTLE
Balmoral 1989 14.0 x 20.1 cm Page 50

18 VIEW OF BALMORAL
Monaltrie 1990 21.5 x 29.0 cm Page 50

19 LOOKING TOWARDS DUBH LOCH
Balmoral 1989 20.1 x 28.3 cm Page 52

20 VIEW TOWARDS SANDY LOCH FROM BRIG O'DEE
Dee Valley 1988 17.0 x 24.2 cm Page 54

21 ALLT-NA-GIUBHSAICH LODGE
Balmoral 1986 6.4 x 11.8 cm Page 56

22 ALLT-NA-GIUBHSAICH
Balmoral 1985 16.5 x 34.0 cm Page 58

23 LOCHNAGAR FROM INVERCAULD PARK
Dee Valley 1989 11.8 x 17.5 cm Page 60

24 LOCHNAGAR
Balmoral 1990 14.2 x 23.7 cm Page 62

25 VIEW OF LOCHNAGAR
Auchtavan 1990 17.7 x 25.2 cm Page 64

26 VIEW OF LOCHNAGAR
Balmoral 1989 15.1 x 24.1 cm Page 66

27 ALLT-NA-GIUBHSAICH, LOCHNAGAR BEYOND
Balmoral 1991 17 x 24.5 cm Page 66

28 VIEW TOWARDS LOCHNAGAR
Balmoral 1988 16.5 x 24.1 cm Page 68

29 BEN AVON FROM THE GELDER COTTAGE
Balmoral 1990 16.1 x 19.3 cm Page 70

30 BEN AVON FROM GLEN GELDER
Balmoral 1990 20.0 x 23.9 cm Page 70

31 LOOKING TOWARDS THE SPITTAL OF GLEN MUICK
Inchnabobart 1990 14.0 x 24.3 cm Page 72

32 LOOKING TOWARDS LOCH MUICK
Inchnabobart 1990 13.9 x 23.6 cm Page 74

33 GLEN MUICK FROM THE SPITTAL OF GLEN MUICK
Inchnabobart 1990 17.2 x 24.6 cm Page 76

34 HOUSE
Sutherland 1988 16.5 x 24.1 cm Page 78

35 VIEW OF DEE VALLEY AND INVERCAULD
Ballochbuie Forest 1988 9.5 x 12.0 cm Page 80

36 VIEW DOWN THE DEE VALLEY TOWARDS BALMORAL
Invercauld Castle 1988 14.2 x 15.5 cm Page 82

37 LOOKING TOWARDS MAR LODGE IN THE RAIN
Dee Valley 1988 11.9 x 17.2 cm Page 84

THE AUTHOR'S ACKNOWLEDGEMENTS

With special thanks to:
Richard Aylard, The Duke and Duchess of Devonshire, Giles Gordon, Derek Hill, Judith Hill,
Genevieve Holmes, Alan Kilkenny, Peter and Cathryn Kuhfeld, Kiloran McGrigor, Peter Munk,
Michael Pearman, Hugh and Emilie van Cutsem, John Ward

First Edition

First published in Great Britain in 1991 by Little, Brown and Company (UK) Ltd,
Beacon House, 30 North End Road, London W14 0SH

ISBN 0-316-88886-9 (UK)
A CIP catalogue record for this book is available from the British Library

ISBN 0-8212-1881-6 (U.S. and Canada)
Library of Congress Catalog Card Number 91-55275
Library of Congress Cataloging-in-Publication information is available.

Designed by Trickett and Webb Limited

Watercolour photography by Prudence Cumming Associates Limited
Still-life photography by Carol Sharp
Portrait of HM Queen Elizabeth The Queen Mother by Michael Plomer/Country Life Books
Colour separations, printing, and binding by Amilcare Pizzi S.p.A., Milan, Italy

Published simultaneously in the United States of America by Bulfinch Press,
an imprint and trademark of Little, Brown and Company (Inc.),
and in Canada by Little, Brown & Company (Canada) Limited

PRINTED IN ITALY